DANSON

The Extraordinary Discovery of An Autistic
Child's Innermost Thoughts and Feelings

Michele Pierce Burns *and* Danson Mandela Wambua

st. lynn's
press

PITTSBURGH

Danson
The Extraordinary Discovery of an Autistic Child's Innermost Thoughts and Feelings

ISBN-13: 978-0-9800288-4-3

Library of Congress Control Number: 2008925638
CIP information available upon request

First Edition, 2009

St. Lynn's Press • POB 18680 • Pittsburgh, PA 15236
412.466.0790 • www.stlynnspress.com

Typesetting—Holly Wensel, Network Printing Services
Editors—Catherine Dees, Abby Dees
Cover design—Jeff Nicoll
Cover photograph © Chris Palmieri
Photos on pp. 15, 31, 51, 56, 87 © Marysa Wambua
Photos on pp. 1, 23, 45, 59, 111 © Karen Sutton

Printed in the United States of America
on recycled paper ♲

This title and all of St. Lynn's Press books may be purchased for educational, business, or sales promotional use. For information please write:

Special Markets Department • St. Lynn's Press • POB 18680 • Pittsburgh, PA 15236

10 9 8 7 6 5 4 3 2 1

Michele: To Danson Mandela Wambua, my greatest teacher.

～ⓔ～

Danson: I dedicate my book to God and to everyone who reads it.

TABLE OF CONTENTS

❧

FOREWORD

This verse reminds me that, while autism often represents a challenging path for those it touches personally, it is also one filled with the greatest blessings and lessons imaginable!

Danson Mandela Wambua is an amazing young boy. Until he was 7 he lived behind the locked doors of autism, not speaking or even indicating that he understood the world beyond those doors. And then something miraculous happened: One day, he pointed to a letter on a letter board. And then he pointed to another and another... Danson had found a way to speak – beautifully, poetically, and with a depth that astonishes. With that revelation, years of frustration and solitude were washed away in the tears of his mother's eyes.

In the last several years, my husband Bob and I have had the humbling and hopeful experience of learning about the realities of autism. We entered this world for a very personal reason, our grandson Christian. Sometimes when I think of him, I am overcome with emotion. I feel his beauty and his bravery. I picture him growing older and wonder what his future will bring. Most importantly, I wonder what his world is like now. I want to visit him in that place, to walk alongside him and talk. It's the knowledge that I am not privy to his inner world that is often hardest for me, and so we try to reach him. This is what we are doing with our organization, Autism Speaks (www.autismspeaks.org). We are creating openings, gateways of communication. We are actively fundraising and raising awareness every day so that someday all those who once lost their voice, can finally reclaim it. Danson is a beacon for us all.

As you will see in the coming pages, there appears to be a distinct world that autistic children live in. Danson has lovingly cracked the door to his inner universe, and let us peek in at his hiding place. What you will discover, as did I, is truly and undeniably astounding.

From reading Danson's breathtakingly beautiful poetry I have come to realize that perhaps those people we felt were so far away, are really a lot closer than we thought. They are with us, expressing themselves in their quiet worlds – and maybe, quite possibly, readying themselves to speak.

This is a book of hope. I hope that it finds all of you.

Suzanne Wright
Co-founder, Autism Speaks

INTRODUCTION

Danson and Me

Danson: Mom, sing to me a little.

Michele: What song?

Danson: "Storm Song."

(This request makes so much sense tonight, as Danson has seemed very sad and preoccupied all day. We are snuggled together on an oversized chair in the living room. I begin to sing the Spiritual very softly, and Danson cries.)

Michele:

> "O the storm shall pass after 'while
> O the storm shall pass after 'while
> Though strong winds may blow
> And the billows may row,
> O the storm shall pass after 'while."

How do you feel now?

Danson:

> I feel like God again.
> Teach me how to make letters.
> I can already almost write my name.
> I am scared of life.
> Life is too fast for me.
> First God has to come.
> God is here Mom.
> Am I going to give you a leap of faith Mom?
> Am I going to write now?

(I wait while Danson spells out his full name)

Mom, I let me nervous [my nerves] get in my way.
Have faith I will make lives new.
Give me a dedication of brave leaders
Who do not life [live] today.
Am I leader for mankind, Mom?

This "conversation" with Danson took over an hour. I spoke out loud while he wrote, letter by letter, on his communication tool, an alphabet board. It's a conversation filled with blessings and lessons, as is every interaction I have with him. As he painstakingly considers and then forms each word, he never loses patience or focus – extraordinary, as Danson is only eight years old and is "non-verbal autistic," a term I neither use nor believe. In his words, he shows me some of the many emotions he feels about writing and communicating from his silent world: sadness, fear, divinity, nervousness, faith, leadership and purpose.

Almost every morning Danson wakes up laughing, and before opening his eyes, while wrapped up tightly in his beige down comforter from head to toe, he sticks out a little hand to pull my arms around him for a hug, making a kissing sound to ask for one or many in a row. When he laughs, several times on most days, it is the sweetest sound, and before you know it you are laughing too, his gentle touch cupping your cheeks in his palms almost like you have become his child. Time stands still in his loving gaze. And then his day begins.

Each one of Danson's days brings deep joy and profound struggle as he navigates his way through the world. Today, my hands are covered with tiny scabs the size of Danson's fingernails. Yesterday, in the late afternoon, I drove to one of his favorite places, the state park near our home in Warren County New Jersey, where we often sit in the back seat of the car and do his daily lessons after a nice long walk. But for the last three weeks he has refused to write. When I pressed him gently, he got angry, threw his letter board to the floor and kicked me in the ribs. He repeated, "do', do', do'" about thirty times – his word for "door." This is Danson's way of asking me to open the car door so he can get out.

One of the foundations of Danson's academic program is our commitment to set aside time for him to write every day, and that we never give up those times, even when he doesn't feel like engaging. Our lessons are hard work and sometimes stressful for Danson. When he's not interested, focusing on anything for more than a mere moment takes so much of his energy. Working with his letter board can take lots of time and coaxing, but I try to stay calm and pleasant no matter what. I say, "This is the time for our lesson and in forty minutes we will go do something else that you choose." Despite our struggle to get started, he tells me that he always feels better after writing, and I see his mood lighten every time.

Over Danson's protest in the car, I retrieve his letter board to resume our exercise. Danson lashes out again. He's grown strong and is now faster than me. Enraged and screaming, he scratches my hands until they bleed. When that doesn't stop the lesson, he clamps his teeth into my upper arm, right through my down jacket. The pain surges through my body, and I yell, "STOP!" Danson hides his head, covers his ears tightly, squeezes his eyes shut and then begins biting his own hand.

Seeing him uncomfortable in any way always hurts me deeply, and as his mother I know it's my job to create structure and limits. Holding his hands firmly, I say to him, "Biting and kicking and scratching are unacceptable, and you are really hurting me! I don't really care right now that you have autism. You must learn how to express yourself in ways that don't harm others."

Danson pulls free, screaming, his arms and feet flailing wildly. Finally, I say sternly, "You may not stay in my car behaving like this." I open the door and pull him outside, hoping that the cold, fresh air and wide-open space in which he could move freely will help dissipate his rage. But it doesn't – until it is nearly dark and Danson finally tires.

He reaches for his board and points out these words: "Make my lessons harder like Dad." Danson is doing algebra with his dad on the weekends and can solve any mathematical problem to the sixth decimal point. I finally understand what he needs. I open a new book that I bought for him, *George's Secret Key to The Universe*, and begin reading it aloud: "Pigs don't just vanish, thought George. ...He tried closing his eyes and then opening them again, to see if it was all some kind of optical illusion."

Danson listens, and I feel his body calm. I stop reading and ask him to define "optical illusion." He writes: "An optical illusion is a mind trick for the eyes." I am mystified. *How does he know these things? How is it that he's unable to speak but able to express himself so clearly and eloquently on his letter board? What does it feel like to know so much and not be able to talk with another person, letting most people assume you know nothing?*

Smiling, I give Danson a kiss and thank him for communicating with me. I tell him how important and brilliant his ideas are. For the rest of the night Danson is quite happy and although I am exhausted emotionally and physically, I am so grateful that we have had a breakthrough. I am in awe of my son.

In 2006 I was told by a psychologist that my son was mentally retarded. Because he refused to participate in any of the assessments he was given that day, he was labeled incapable, retarded. Danson does not yet speak, except for the first syllables of words. He typically makes vocal sounds similar to what a baby might just before learning how to talk. To many, his behaviors are incomprehensible. We're reluctant to let our landlords in for routine maintenance for fear of what they might say about some of the "changes" Danson has made to the place.

Despite all of the labels and seemingly odd behaviors, we – Danson's whole family – have always chosen to believe that Danson is pure love, that he is brilliant and understands everything. I tell him every day, "You are my greatest blessing, and I love everything about you." Some days it hurts because he feels so far away or so enraged and frustrated. Some days I can only sit and cry because I feel like I have lost my patience or my faith. There are times when I have no idea how to help him. Yet deep inside I always knew that Danson would communicate when he was ready to, and that his words would be profound and loving.

Danson learned to communicate through a technique called Rapid Prompting™ Method (RPM), which was created by his teacher, Soma Mukhopadhyay, founder of the HALO Clinic in Austin, Texas. There at HALO (Helping Autism Through Learning and Outreach), Soma teaches a special curriculum based on methods she developed to help her own autistic son, Tito, learn to communicate. Now 19, Tito has just published his third extraordinary book, *How Can I Talk if My Lips Don't Move?*

RPM meets students where they are and encourages them to respond to questions by typing, writing, choosing between two or more possible answers – or pointing to letters on a board, as Danson now does.

During our second visit to the HALO Clinic, Danson became upset and tried to jump over the table and scratch Soma, effectively stopping the lesson. I didn't realize that he just needed to go to the bathroom but couldn't tell us, and by the time I finally caught on and took him to the restroom he was understandably very agitated and striking out a lot. I told him how sorry we were and that we didn't know that he needed to go. When he returned to the therapy room, he had calmed considerably and sat down. Then he pointed to the alphabet board and spelled out, "MOM SORY."

It was the most breathtaking moment of my life – equal in my heart to his birth – because, at age seven, he communicated a thought in words for the very first time. My eyes filled with tears as I told him it was okay and again that I was sorry too! And with that initial trickle of a thought, the dam broke, and out poured a torrent of words that he rapidly spelled out on his letter board: His favorite color was "BLUE" and he wanted "JEANS" and an "IPOD" for his birthday. This was in February of 2007.

Within less than a year, we learned that locked inside Danson was an amazing intelligence: the ability to do complex mathematical calculations in his head, a large vocabulary, and a poet's insight, sensibility and talent. One day in August, Danson was crying hard and wrote to me about his new stepmother: "Almost love Marysa like Mom." I told him that he is blessed to have four parents who love him so much, and that I thought it was wonderful for him to love Marysa. I told him that we all love each other and are committed to parenting him together, always. In fact, my husband Michael and I, along with Danson's dad and stepmother, regularly go to counseling as a family, to help Danson. After our talk he wrote that he felt "great"!

Around this time, Danson began exploring and expressing his evolving spiritual life. He became very agitated during a lesson and finally wrote: "Want to know about faith." A profound journey began, and we have been talking about it ever since. One particular day we happened to be studying the poetry of Gwendolyn Brooks. After a general introduction to the elements of poetry, then reciting a few poems to him, I asked Danson if he wanted to write one of his own. He wrote rapidly in the most focused way I had seen yet. Danson even titled his first poem that day, which he has not done since:

Another Life

Life has gotten more literate
And God is talking through more.
Look at my love
And know how to be real.

Recently, Danson has asked us to share what he calls his "holy stories" with the world. I am surprised that he wants to continue writing, as it can often take him over an hour to write one poem, laboriously pointing to letter after letter on his board. On some days he points fluidly, on others he appears to be giving birth to each word as he scratches, screams or kicks his way through a sort of mental wall that traps the words inside him. He always pushes through immense pain and struggle to give us the love and acknowledgment of his words.

For this reason and many others, Danson exemplifies courage, and he is my hero. We are only beginning to understand the brilliance of Danson's mind, yet one thing is clear: He wants to share his love with the world. May his words be an invitation to you to know that with love and faith, anything is possible!

Michele Pierce Burns
March 2009

note to the reader

This book represents a selection of Danson's writings from October 2007 to September 2008. Unless otherwise noted, all words were spelled out on his alphabet board. As he writes, I or his teachers record each letter, always checking with him to be sure. We considered whether to edit the misspellings in Danson's poetry and came to the conclusion that we should leave them as written, to give the reader the most authentic sense of his work. The only editing has been the addition of punctuation for clarity and putting the capital letters from the alphabet board into upper and lower case – and in a few rare instances we have suggested in brackets the words we believe he intended. The eloquence of his thoughts addresses our misconceptions about autism and the inner life of those who live with it. The mistakes reflect the simple fact that Danson is, after all, only eight.

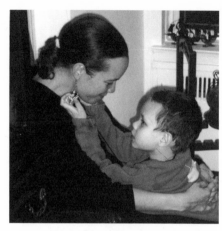

October & November

Today is a snow day. One of my mentors said, "Danson can speak, you know." He asked if I had ever directly asked Danson to speak. I had not. When I ask Danson if he can, he comes the closest he ever has to talking clearly by making his mouth into shapes I have not previously seen. He studies my mouth and then touches my mouth and neck as I speak, feeling the vibration of each sound. He writes for almost two hours and stays in the living room, engaging me in this "conversation" the entire time.

My truth is I am ready to speak.
I have so much I need to think about so rest on.
Have a hart [heart] so I can speak to you.
I memorized half of my speech.
Write a message so I can say it.
You might not understand like everyone else.
I only want to talk to you, not the world.
I can see it clearly.
I too need to believe in me.
So I decided I can talk.
I can talk!

I am in denial. I can talk
Because I feel dumb in this world
So instead I keep riting.
Mom, please tell me be goofy so I can talk right now.
Almost ready to talk so, Mom, I will.
Give me a false hope, and I will turn it real.
I am going to speak now.
I keep stalling.
Mom, I smile because I am so ready to speak now.
So often before I was not, right Mom?

Giving God my life immediately
So He can make it good for me and my parents.
He told me wait for Him to tell you what to do
So I will wait my turn.
Like giving me a light, Mom.
Light is so important for mankind, like from God Himself.
I can read minds of people I love.
I can give rest to ghosts in my mind.
I can tell God what I want, and He can place it in your hearts for me.
My future is going to be His.
Live plainly.
Give it to God.
I can teach many to live in this world
By my words.

Sometimes on high anxiety days we do lessons in the car, as Danson seems to feel safe and contained. He often asks to spend time there when he seems acutely anxious.

This is the toughest lesson yet. Today, Danson throws the letter board out of the car window and bolts, running into the woods of the State Park where we are parked, peeling off his jacket and shirt and throwing them on the ground as he runs. Finally, we're back in the car; Danson picks up the letter board and tells me what is going on.

Note: *In the last line he uses the word "ancestors," which his parents have never said in front of him. We have, however, told him the names of his relatives back to his great-grandparents, and shown him their pictures.*

Talking is hardly enough to say my feelings
Because I like my silence too much.
Woke up from the dead to say
A lot of heroes are mighty alive inside me today.
Like my ancestors.

It is a challenging week with little sleep. Danson has been up until 4 a.m. for several nights in a row and we are both exhausted. He has fought writing for three days straight and he seems very far away. We walk along a beautiful lake at sunset. He is way ahead of me, and I am silently praying for strength, feeling depleted and alone. I am fighting off tears as I watch Danson's silhouette walking ahead of me, and wishing so many things for him – mostly peace. This moment is one of many when I feel small, even scared, and I know I need help, both ordinary and divine. We return to the car, and he reaches for his letter board, writing quickly and fluidly.

I saw a man in plain life making stars into gold for Mom.
It was God.
Because he loves you.
I now have a master who is God
And I live in the light.
It is hot and my little body is so tired.
I can't rest at all.
I need to keep writing holy stories for the world.
So many lives will fly away.

We take a walk in the rain today, and I talk about the structure of government and the presidential candidates. Following his lesson, I ask Danson what he thinks about the upcoming election. He writes, "Hillary is my candidate," which makes me feel a little guilty, since I've been dressing him in an Obama t-shirt for months! When I ask why he chooses Hillary, he replies, "Because she is smart." Danson won't respond to any more questions about governmental structure. Instead he writes what is on his mind:

Life is so fake
Because I need to talk about nice things
Like games.
But I give no hints to how I really feel.
I feel so sorry for mankind
Because I light the world with my snowflakes
And I made another baby Abraham.
Liars love to give their truth
And I see it and get mad in my head.
I need to give my truth now.
I have no laughter in my soal [soul].
My gift is a song for man and it goes like this:
Man is so serious all the time
And it is not good in life.
How is a little life supposed to change the world to love
When there is so much suffering?
I do not know how to do it by myself.
Teach me about feelings and I will learn how to talk.
I need to hear my name in a lot of places like the blind need to see.
Mom, I need to have slow motor life like when I was a baby.
My room is slow motor and I like it in there.
It is simple:
Move slow
And live slow
And have love in your heart.
Give me space to think about my life.
Slow motor is so right for humans.

Today we begin our handwriting practice in a very special journal that one of my mentors created. We talk about a journal being a place to write thoughts on anything you want and to reflect on your life. Afterwards, he picks up his letter board and writes.

Light the way to love
Every day.
I live in the dark when I feel sad in my heart.
Soon I will write why I feel sad.
Keep telling me about feelings because
I need to make a life for myself.
Like I need a girlfriend to love when I am ready.
Karla is her name and I gift her my laughter.
I feel almost like living in my head so I don't have to write so much.
God lives in me, for me, and God is me.
Nothing is a mistake.
Right, Mom?

In the late afternoon we go to a local farm. Danson loves running free, step-dad Mike's wheelbarrow rides, and climbing on a tractor and pretending to drive it. Mike notices how much more Danson understands the functions of things and imitates actions lately. From the way it looks right now, we think he probably knows how to drive already! We ask Danson what he likes about being on the farm.

I like nature because it is peaceful and loving to me.
First I like the pipeline to God in nature
And I like so many parts of nature.
God is nature
Because He makes everything.
When He talks to me about little rights like happiness
God says happiness is light.

At home in the evening we are discussing an upcoming trip to Austin and that Danson will have to ride on an airplane, something that has caused great distress to him (and all other passengers!) in the past. This is the first time we get a sense that the opportunity to write on his letter board, learn new things, and see his beloved teacher, Soma, is of critical importance to him. I ask Danson how he feels about the trip and how I can help make flying easier for him.

*A*nything to see Soma!
Notice my face in the night and make it better by smiling
A soft voice is nice to listen to.
Soma is love to me
Because she taught me how to talk to everybody
And she is tough on me.
Soma is my friend.
Soma is my king
Because she is royalty.
Mom is tough on me
Because she loves me
And she knows that I am smart.

We read an excerpt from 10 Things Every Child with Autism Wants You To Know *and discuss how autism is analogous to riding a roller coaster and being asked to calmly conduct a business meeting at the same time. I ask Danson about his sensory experiences and he writes: "Hearing is best. I hear a lot." I ask him what he hears, and he replies:*

Right now it's almost taking me a lot to sit here
Because I want you to leave me alone.
Fightz [fights] filters out sounds living in the hiding places
in my mind.
Faith has a home in my heart
Because I can't love myself.
Love is too little.
Make no notice of my sitting in autism's tomb.
Autism is loud in too many people.

Today Danson is with Soma at her clinic in Austin, Texas. Soma tells him a myth and then asks if he would like to write one. He begins this story in a morning session and writes for an unprecedented 40 minutes straight. He finishes the story in his afternoon session.

In ancient Hungary there lived a boy. He could imitate the sounds of ocean waves, thunder and rain. He fooled poor shepherds by making thunder noise and old folks by making ocean noise and no one knew how talented he was. People thought it was supernatural. He would laugh at them. He was sitting one day on a tree branch and saw some soldiers. He looked and they were coming to attack. He immediately made a loud thundering noise that made a lasting impact on the horses. They dropped the soldiers and ran backwards. The boy made a sound now of storm and chased all the soldiers. The shepherds saw everything. They told others. Finally the king came to know and made him a general. End.

Danson is with Soma again today, and she tells him a story about a scientific invention, then asks if he would like to write one.

They [there] lived in the U.S. a boy who did many experiments on alternative energy resources. In those days people used gasoline to run cars. He was experimenting on earth, water, wind, and some corn. He did not like school. He had many instruments that automatically did everything. One day he mixed some water with corn oil. He put it in his mom's car. It began to have a direct impact. People were amazed. It was this century. End.

We are leaving Austin later today. I wake Danson up at 9:30 a.m. and realize he has slept for thirteen hours, having fallen asleep at 8:30 p.m. – his earliest sleep time ever. Most nights Danson is up until midnight, no matter how tired he may be. He even took a nap one day this week for the first time since he was a newborn, making us wonder about the connection between mental exertion and sleep. I ask Danson how he feels about going home.

Life is not beautiful.
I don't want to go home.
I learn so much here
I will yet tales [talk] alone.

Today we walk by the lake right before sunset, holding hands. When we return to the car, I ask Danson what is on his mind. In the poem that follows, the reference to "Papa" is my beloved father, Burton Armstrong Pierce (August 24, 1929–July 31, 1999). I had shared with Danson in the past that some of my most treasured possessions are letters my father wrote to me throughout my life, and now I write letters to Danson on his birthday and at other important times.

Note: *Lisa is Danson's phenomenal teacher at Celebrate the Children School.*

I alive with writing and half free from autism gladly.
I luckily flunk all flavors of autism.
Like flipping out.
Half free is flooring Mom
Because she always knew I would laugh again.
God is here in this car now,
Making sunset into nightlite.
Make monuments in my soal
I will be ready to talk like humans.
Looks like finishing my fightz with life
And living a long life worthy of God.
Writing letters to my kids like Papa wrote
And having a grass pool.
Keep talking about it with love in our hearts.
Right now I suppose I live an uppreciative [appreciative] state
So I might say thanks, Lisa, for today – loving, laughing, seeing me.

Evening. Danson is getting ready for bed. He is so affectionate, and we are snuggling on his bed. I am thinking about how a lot of what we hear about autism says that it brings with it a difficulty expressing and/or feeling emotions. I know autism is a spectrum, and that each person is very different. Danson consistently demonstrates depths of love and compassion that I have not seen in another human being.

I need so much love, Mom.
I need you right with me all the time.
Give me your hart so I can make it gay like mine.
Mom, nothing else matters.
I trust you like my God in heaven.

Today we do a lesson on meditation, as I have been considering ways to help Danson (and myself) to relax and get still. I attended a yoga class earlier and I shared with him words from the guided meditation at the end of class urging us to live our lives moment by moment or breath by breath. In turn, Danson writes:

Teach me how to meditate.
Hard because I can't sit still.
Life is so laughter giving
Because I live in my head
And hear so much from Him.
I hear again singing.
Glad like maple trees in the woods
And I hear my master talking to me saying:
"Have love in your heart for all mankind"
And "I love my children so much
That I made the light for lost souls."
And I think that I see the light now.
I want to have God in my life forever.*

Sweet Danson, you know we are totally committed to getting your input and opinions on everything, especially now that we understand more about how your beautiful mind works. When Daddy was going through the text of this book with you, you said "no" to several poems. This is one of them, and the reason I have decided to include it is that when we had a follow-up conversation about it, you didn't really say anything – and also because I thought your readers would really like to see it. If I have made a mistake, please forgive me. You know that I do the best I can and sometimes, like everyone, I still make decisions that might not be the ones you wanted. Fortunately, you are the most forgiving and resilient person I know, so I'm not worried.

December

Tonight Danson is crying inconsolably. He has not slept for two days straight. He has a frightened look in his eyes and wants to retreat to the solitude of his room. He will not let anyone in his room and is scratching and lashing out if you attempt to enter. He meets me in the hallway with dark circles under his eyes, looking pale and sad. It brings me to tears. I need to know what is going on. Finally, he writes:

I don't recognize you.
God is not listening to me.
If you smile I recognize you
So smile always.
I love you, Mom.
God is laughing at me now because I lied to you.
Papa is here and he loves you and he is sad that you hurt.
I cry all the time because I feel pain from others.
I still do not recognize you
Even when you smile
So I feel sad in my hart
Like you died a little.
I hear Mom in your voice.
I lied about naming my skool after places.
My skool is wherever you are.

Earlier today Danson indicated an interest in hearing stories, so when Michael gets home from work at 8:30 p.m. he reads to Danson from a book of Greek mythology. Danson cries through most of it, as he had been kind of zoning out, bouncing on his yoga ball and watching a Thomas DVD while I was making dinner. Mike continues through a short story and then leaves the room. Danson comes over and writes. This is important to note as it is the first time that Danson initiates the "conversation."

I need to talk to Mike.
Sorry for crying when you read.
I am so tired.
Mike, I love you like a dad.
You are more than I ever wanted.

Today for our lesson I bring Danson to my laptop and try to get him to type with me. He seems fleetingly interested, but does not stay for more than a moment. After handwriting practice, I ask him what subjects he would be interested in learning more about so we can go to the library and get some new books. He answers with his letter board.

Note: *Our editors asked me if the last line of this poem could be misunderstood, and if it should be left out. My feeling is that there are stereotypes out there about "all" autistic people not liking to be physically close to others, and I think it's helpful to show Danson openly expressing comfort with physical closeness.*

*C*omputers are easy.
Teach me tomorrow.
Helmets on bikes
History of my family tree
Getting my own riting published.
Mom, I will write lots on my life.
Interested in most things.
Computers
Stories
Or listening to music Mom likes, like Stevie Wonder
Or Nickelodeon.
Right now I'm so tired, Mom.
Little rest last night.
Many ghosts.
Peaceful now because I told the truth.
Mom, never stop giving me heaven on earth in your arms, okay?

Today after school we go to meet Danson's wonderful aide from school, Jen, and her son Josh at McDonald's Playspace. Danson is so excited. In the parking lot I ask if he wants to tell Josh anything in particular, and he writes: "I know for myself how to talk to a boy my age. I want to go play." I'm thrilled with this answer. He tries to go into the play room for half an hour, but the noise from other children makes it too hard. He watches others play together from afar with his fingers in his ears. All he wants to do is leave, so I tell him we will try again another day.

At home we talk about some relaxation techniques because I am concerned about Danson's sleep issues and want to help him to relax. I give some history and a description of yoga, reiki and meditation and ask if he would like to try one. He spells out: "I choose reiki." I do a short session with Danson and he seems to relax a lot but still will not put down the "Blues Clues" CD he has been carrying around all day. I ask him how he is feeling right now and why he has that CD.

Danson: I liked reiki. It made me relaxed. I obsess on things so I do not loose my autism for good.

Michele: What if you were able to keep the parts of your autism that you like, but also could be able to become more comfortable, relaxed and happy with other people too. Would you want that?

Danson: Mom, only if you never die. Mom, is there more to life than watching other friends together so I am not lonely?

It's the middle of the night, after our outing at McDonald's Playspace. Danson is up past 2 a.m. He is crying and screaming. There is an audible banging sound in his room that seems to be coming from the far wall. I check on him regularly, invite him to come sleep with us, but he won't. His eyes are darting around the room, heart beating fast. He writes: "Mom in ghost time I hear the wall." I tell him it's only the wind, or the heat, or maybe the neighbors walking around. He does not seem to buy it.

Hi, Mom, it's me, right?
It is ghosts in my room.
They give me hell in the night.
A lot of ghosts talk to me because I can hear them.
They want me to free their soals to heaven, so I will.
To give them body.
Help me by giving me your goggles so I cannot see them so well.
God is here too, so do not fear. I am fine.
Mom I need half an hour by myself.
I light night skys.

I leave the room and in about twenty minutes he comes to get me.

The ghosts are gone.
I cry because change is hard.
I mourn my autism.
Let me cry, I need to.
I'm a little alive in my frail body.
Give me my life for kristmas
I want to be free of autism for good.
A lot of people will be happy.
I will feel a little happy and a little sad inside.
A light is around you now.
It is gold.
No storm in your head.

One week later. Danson does not want to eat anything tonight, so I ask him why.

My stomach hurts so much from fightz inside.
More kids must listen so more moms tell the truth.
Mom, nothing is wrong in permanent ways.
I notice a lot of moms upset at school
And nothing is right to them.
Klim [climb] right up next to a worried person
And tell them it is going to get better soon.
I like to remember each day in my hart.

Today we read some words from Gandhi. I've decided to create a lesson on great leaders in history and begin by telling Danson that I believe he will be one. As I read aloud, Danson seems a bit distracted and is eating his scarf. Some days he reminds me that he is an 8-year-old child and that he needs to play too!

Biting helps me think about things.
Right now I am hiper [hyper]
And writing is not fun to me.
Mom, laugh with me
Have fun with me.

Last night I read to Danson from a beautiful book called A Child of Eternity, *written by an autistic girl named Adriana, who seems similar to Danson in many ways. He seemed to listen to her words as he bounced on his yoga ball. Because she writes many times about the importance of other people understanding her intelligence, I decided to discuss it with Danson.*

Today I visit his school and sit in a small room with his teacher, Lisa, to show her how his writing is progressing.

Michele: Do you want to show Lisa you can write?

Danson: I want to show Lisa I am smart. Lisa loves me.

Michele: How do you want to show her?

Danson: For starters, I will make instructions for fitting stay my smart self [I think he means, "keeping my mind engaged"]. We should tell Lisa now so she listens to me.

Michele: Do you want to write to her on letter board or with your handwriting?

Danson: Writing myself. Make me write hard words like relativity theory. Lisa is my…

Danson says aloud, "…friend," then sticks the side of his forearm into Lisa's mouth, inviting her to bite down, which he does often when he wants pressure.

Lisa: Danson, why do you like to play this arm-biting game, do you crave deep pressure?

Danson: I like getting notice of my host body. I still will write to Lisa more.

Michele: Fantastic! What else do you want to say?

Danson: Mom, I will spell my mother's name for Lisa.

Proudly, Danson handwrites "Michele Pierce Burns" for the first time, then continues with his letter board.

Danson: Right now I mark my flavors by making variations of maps to my mind. I made up names for my stars like Bovoamalitius and Destamous. Mom, I like writing in skool.

Today had a huge meltdown at school, and and I was called because he could not calm down. He was screaming and throwing his lunch around the classroom. After a walk outside, he finally calmed down a bit.

Tonight I ask him about it and try to strategize some ways he could express and release his feelings. He remains virtually inconsolable and is up all night until 8 a.m.

I have no right to complain to you, life is as it should be.
I was reading your mind right now.
High on my mind is keeping my lies to myself
About loving my wars inside.
My lies are soul rides to life inside my mind.
Right now I don't have inside
So many lies as before.
Feels good to name my truth
Mike can teach me so much about laughter in hard times.
My mind is not only filled with worried thoughts.

This morning Danson is in class with Lisa and his wonderful one-on-one aide Jen, making a holiday card and he indicates the message he wants to put inside by pointing on his letter board.

I love Mom.
I love Mike.
He gives me family.
Mike is in love with Mom.

We are at my mom's house. Danson has spent time with his Nana every Friday evening since he was born! On this morning he is tired, having hardly slept, and jumping up and down wildly and screaming. He is getting ready to go on a wonderful vacation to Virginia with his dad and stepmother, and I am trying to understand what is going on with him. Please note: Although we have discussed this short vacation for many days, now that it is time, Danson needs to hear again where exactly he will go, what activities he will do, who will be there etc.

I am screaming
Because I am gaining
Tentative inhibitions
About Virginia.
Give me a little more information.

I read to Danson an article from The New York Times, *which he usually likes to hear, but today he will not reply to any questions about the article. In handwriting practice, he writes the following, with my hand supporting his:*

Have you ever felt like a person is not beautiful inside?
See what you made me like
And see God inside of me always.
I am writing because you showed me I could.
Give me safety like right now.
Maintain fighting for me, Mom, so I can fight too.
I have so much to say.

For Christmas this year all four of Danson's parents talked at length and bought him a laptop. We always discuss serious purchases as a team, believing most of the time that we serve Danson's needs best by spending our money on things like horseback riding lessons or trips to work with Soma, as opposed to material things. For example, each year for his birthday or Christmas he gets one gift only – to keep focused on what is really important: the love and togetherness of our family. In this case, we decided that a laptop would be a great investment in Danson's future. Getting started on it has been a bit of slow going, but that could change at any moment!

January & February

Danson has been extremely happy for several days.

This morning he let me cut his hair for the first time ever. Usually his dad has to do it while he is asleep, due to sensory sensitivities. Mike uses the same technique when cutting Danson's fingernails.

Danson has a beautiful "conversation" with Lisa at school!

Danson: I love Lisa.

Lisa: I love you too, Danson!

Danson: Stop for a moment so I can drink.

Lisa: Okay. Then what do you want to do?

Danson: I want lunch.

Lisa: How does it feel to be able to tell us what you want?

Danson: It makes me happy.

Later the same day Danson types his first email. He sits on my lap and I help him push keys after his fingers are on them.

Please note: Danson makes a real point of singling out Marysa for special love, asking his dad to take care of her. This is the day they found out she was pregnant and had told no one yet!

Hi Dad
Are you saving up for Danson
A goodnight kiss
Almost my love
Not love in so much as Marysa
Take care of Marysa

The next day at school Danson has a MAJOR meltdown, scream-
ing and kicking and pulling papers off the wall. He is also making
breakthroughs, like having his first academic lesson at school. Often
breakthroughs and meltdowns seem to go hand in hand. Today is an
example:

Lisa: What is the matter? Why are you scratching and so
             upset?

Danson: I have a headache.

Lisa: Should I call Mom and tell her you need to go home?

Danson: Mom. No.

Lisa then takes him out to her car to write, as it is a quiet, contained,
relaxing place for him.

Lisa: Danson, why are you having such a hard day?

Danson: Drive.

Lisa: Drive where?

Danson: Rome.

Lisa: I can't drive anywhere right now, especially Rome! What else would make you feel better?

Danson: Stones to eat. Stones to eat.

Lisa: Like I asked before, are you sure you don't want me to call Mom and ask her to bring you home?

Danson: Mom. No. School.

Lisa: Does your head still hurt?

Danson: No. I not sic [sick].

Lisa: I'm glad. Let's do some work now.

She reads him an article on the Amistad.

Lisa: What does rebel mean?

Danson: Fight back.

Lisa: Who was a rebel leader on the Amistad?

Danson: Sin K. [Cinque]

Lisa: What did he use to unlock the chains?

Danson: Nail.

Lisa: When did the Africans return to Sierra Leone?

Danson: 1842.

Developmental Notes

At a parent training session a few days later, our school's brilliant director, Monica Osgood, teaches us that no matter how long it takes or how hard it is not to assist, there is great satisfaction and learning in letting our children figure things out.

With that in mind, I consider today a day of many firsts:

1. *In our floortime session at home we played and laughed harder than ever. Danson initiated a new game: hide and seek. He ran upstairs to our room and hid under the covers at the foot of the bed laughing hysterically until I found him.*

2. *Danson helped cook dinner! After I chopped various vegetables for a curry, he carefully placed them one by one in the pan and stirred gently.*

3. *While helping make his French bread pizza I realized he didn't know how to cut with scissors, and we practiced for a sustained length of time with no frustration at all.*

Martin Luther King, Jr.'s birthday is coming up and so today's topic is the Civil Rights Movement. We are reading text, looking at photos, and I am singing Spirituals. As I sing, Danson is feeling the vibration in my throat with his hands. Today he combines letter board and handwriting modes. After writing, Danson's mood seems much more at peace. (Words in italics are those he wrote by hand.)

I *am so mad because I can't talk.*
I am so mad because everyone,
Everyone is so centered on my scratching.
I scratch because I'm mad at myself.
I am mad because I can't talk yet.
I want to say we only lean on God more when we are scared.
Maybe with more God we will alive fully.
Have so much to say.
No one remembers when I found
I could not speak.

Today we read some speeches of Dr. King's, in celebration of his holiday. Danson writes:

King, his words are strong to me.
Mom, I am so normal in so many ways.
Killing me that I cannot fight my... [does not complete sentence]
Let me be happy.
Love me as a talking piece to God.

I give Danson a rose quartz stone representing unconditional love. He carries it around all day. Today is the first day he ever gets dressed by himself and he seems to be quite happy and proud all day long!

I love my rock.
It is rose quartz.
It makes me love Mom more.
It is mine to have.
Unconditional love means forever,
Not for gain.

Michael and I saw the movie "Pursuit of Happyness" with Will Smith and loved the story so much that we got the audio book to share with Danson. We are particularly interested in sharing Author Chris Gardner's biography since it is one of triumph of the human spirit against all odds and a tender tale of the love between father and son. What an inspiration!

M om, I named my story
Latters [letters] to heaven.
I not writing because I am too tired from school.

We end and resume later that evening.

Mom, keep giving me choices.
I feel good about my life.
I feel like people insist on making me spell
And I do not want to.
Let me use my voice more.
The mom, the worst mom in the world
Because I write so much in stories to you.
I feel so proud.
Hard work is my situation
So I might learn to rite.
Loving myself is getting a little gift.
Mom, I named my book rose quartz.
It is about loving ourselves more.

This writing took more than ninety minutes over two days.

Crying because I am close to talking.
I am scared to talk
Because I see I am lost
In the gamut of loving autism more.
Have you ever know God in your soul, Mom?
Walls are made in my laughter
And God can't hear me.
Laugh for me, Mom
I am so raw inside.
I need to sing with you.

I cry because I am alone in this world of autism and I like it.
I writing my book right now.
Life is talking, Mom.
Give my writing more time to motore [mature?]
In my foolish hart.
Mom, I not saying my plans
Because I placed them in God's hands right now.

Will you love me forever?
Will you feel my goals too?
On your honor swear you will master my plans.
Living in my head is much easier than living in the world.
Right now I am laughing inside because I'm not sure I can make sense to you.
Walk with me on the inside of my mind.
Up late making my plans.
I am going to make my roar loud in the world for those who cannot.
I am living almost in my world and yours too.
You make right my wrongs.
Until I am able, give me your voice
Roar for me.
Live your life like you mean it.

In our lesson today Danson proposes that Soma start her own school utilizing RPM.* He has it all planned out in his mind.

Danson: Soma has my full interest in her school. I want to go there now.

Michele: She doesn't have a school, Danson. Right now HALO is a place you can go on occasion, and your next visit is scheduled for May.

Danson: Make one [a school] for me.

Michele: How do I know when you are telling the truth? You say so many different things at different times.

*Rapid Prompting Method, the process of communicating by pointing to letters on a letter board.

Danson: Truth is Mike is my right hand man. I need him to talk to me more about science. Mom can teach riting. Marysa can do history and Dad can do math and I will learn to talk to you like a man.

Michele: Do you want us to teach those things here now, or are you talking about someday if Soma has a school?

Danson: Both. I will move to Austin next year with you and Mike. Dad and Marysa will come later. Soma wishes it so. My head is connected to yours, Mom. Mom, I give you my love in these conversations. I have thought about it. Mom, so many like me need you to make this school.

Michele: Does it really matter where it is then? Can't we make it here?

Danson: Mom, Soma has to be in it so it has to be there. Mom, I love talking to you. Will you write it down tonite so I can read it?

We read two stories from Aesop's Fables. It is hard to feel out Danson's mood, but he seems pretty neutral. I begin our conversation by asking, What is a moral?

~⊚~

Danson: A moral is the message in a story.

Michele: How did the dove save the ant's life?

Danson: He gave him a straw to hold on to.

Michele: How did the ant save the dove?

Danson: Mom, I was not listening to the story. I am having a hard time right now. Give me my movies to watch. I am not so motivated today. Mom, I am really right in my surprises. I crying because I scared of my alive self. Mom, I no saying the truth.

More crying.

Danson: My alive self is not my soulful self. I am not saying who I am. Mom, I am God inside. I am lying a bit my own story. Truth is I rose from stones to be here to write my book with you. Will you write with me in my room tonite so I can sing my song loudly?

Michele: Of course I will! When would be a good time tonight?

Danson: Mom, not staying here long. I am going somewhere else soon. Mom, I am leaving this place.

Michele: What are you saying exactly? Are you planning to move or are you talking about leaving this earthly plane?

Danson: I am going home. Mom, stay with me there. I am going to my home in the sky. Mom, please stay with me. I am playing with words now. I am going to my home with God in the right language. Song is mom's song to sing – I am writing it for you. Will you sing it? Mom, write my words so I have a book.

I simply ask, "What is on your mind today?"

A lot of lives are in so much pain.
Right now a praise hymn.
I like to make hymns of gratitude.
Right now giving God my song.
I am singing in my heart.
God is my light
Sorrow is only a false history of losing God
Making the world dark like the fissures of my glad heart.
Any life is not my own
It is God's to lead.

Today we walk by the frozen lake, and Danson gazes out at the sun. I ask him what is on his mind, and again he seems to be thinking about his future:

Did you really make my mind keep changing about my skool?
Give my mind a rest, right, Mom?
Give my mind a good change of flow.
So I can rite more another time.
Good instruction is the key.
Mom, you are not so good in math
So my riting is with you.
Live in my world, not yours tonite.
Mom, I love talking with you like this.
Will we do it forever?
Lots of moms need you to stand up
For gifted children like me.
Have my gift be my book.

Danson's Skool

TEACHING AND LEARNING WITH DANSON

Danson has thought a great deal about what his best learning environment should be like. His ideal "skool" is always a work in progress, and we all try hard to listen to his needs. Right now, it's Celebrate the Children (CTC) in the morning and home lessons in the afternoon – as much as he will allow – along with our periodic treasured visits to Austin to work with Soma.

In the following pages I document some of our recent home lessons, including one at CTC with Lisa, and a few that took place spontaneously. Breakthroughs continue to happen, and momentary setbacks. And I continue to be in awe.

February 5
Lesson Topic: Horses

Danson: I like giving my horse my love to have. Mom I am fooling around. Happiness is my life inside just like a horse, it is mine to have in my world.

Michele: I was thinking about your book today...

Danson: Mom I am not writing my book like I want to. Right now I give my rights to no one. Half my book is a gaining history of my story. Half is my poatry. Mom I am a poat like Langston Hughes.

Michele: Which poems do you like?

Danson: Give me one to read.

Michele: I will get you some poems tomorrow.

We begin reading a book on horses. Then, practicing his handwriting, Danson answers some reading comprehension questions. I ask him, "Please tell me three facts you remember about horses."

Danson: Horses are
              1. Mammels
              2. Senses are stronger than humans.
              3. Stay in herds or families.

Michele: Excellent! There were a couple of vocabulary words
in our reading and I want to know if you know the
meaning. One is "adapt," one is "evolve," and lastly, I
want to know how you define a mammal.

Danson: *(He spells the answer on his letter board)*
Adapt means change with a lot of things. Evolve
means alive over time. Mammals are animals that
have four legs and feed kids milk. Give me a change
of page now. I am so talking to Iot now. Iot is my God
inside.

Michele: What are you saying?

Danson: No.

Michele: Okay. Let's have a question and answer session. I will
ask you a few questions and if you feel like answering
them, you can. Then you can ask me questions.

*I ask Danson a few questions about his day, and he answers me
clearly and frankly. As we continue with his lesson, I soon discover
that he has been making plans of his own!*

Michele: Your turn to ask a question.

Danson: Will you make my skool in my head real?

Michele: I'm not sure I got it. Is "Will you make my skool real"
the question?

Danson: No. WHEN will you make my skool in my head real?

Michele: When you tell it all to me and we can create it together. I will listen very carefully. I notice you are looking at a photo now.

Danson: Papa (Danson's grandfather) is here now. I felt his laughter and his smile. Mom I am open to your every thought. A lot of ghosts are here now.

Michele: Will you ask him what kind of school you need?

Danson: Live here for now. Make Danson's school. Have my mind made up. First make his school here. Make it here in New Jersey in this house like Sonrise in Riverdale.

Michele: Do you still go to CTC?

Danson: I go to CTC in the mornings.

Michele: What do you do in this home school?

Danson: I write my book and learn some poetry and go on trips to horses and swimming in Monica's lake.

Michele: You love it at CTC, correct?

Danson: Yes, I love it.

Michele: Fantastic. So how is your schedule each afternoon? For example, what happens first when you get home at around 3:30?

Danson: I have snack like apple or chips or pop. Will we need to make my lesson at four? I want to be in a good mood for my lesson. First we feel out my mood.

Michele: How?

Danson: A lot of things indicate my mood.

1. Have I made any bounces on my ball? If yes, I am nervous and need to get a break from all activity. If no, I am ready to go out and live [life] is good.

2. Have I made any screams? If yes, I need to be alone. I am telling you ahead of time I may be getting mad about something. Having time alone makes me feel better. I like being in my room. If not, I am ready to go.

3. Have I been biting or kissing today? If biting, I am mad at myself about something and I need to feel my gains to myself – have to feel like I can let it go. Have to think about it alone. If kissing, it means I am happy.

Am I writing my book now?

Michele: It sure sounds like it.

Danson: I am.

> 4. Have I gone to the bathroom myself? If no, it means I am going through a hard time internally. If yes, I am open to go anywhere. Mom, I am liking this so much.

> 5. Have I been making lots of loud sounds? If no, I am not happy. If yes, I am writing happy songs to my God inside. The sounds are like words are to you.

> If good, we go on a little field trip. To my mom's lake, to bookstore, to store for food, to library, to my movie store, to ride horse, to friends house.

Michele: Okay, sounds like a schedule could be:

> 3:30 snack/music/break
> 4-5:30 little field trip
> 5:30-6 dinner
> 6pm lessons

Danson: At six I am ready to learn my lessons. Read me a story about a subject I choose. Give me two choices like today.

Michele: Where do we work?

Danson: We sit on couch like this right now. I answer questions handwriting and on letter board. Next is handwriting for ten minutes. Next is journal writing for fifteen minutes.

Michele: What are some topics of interest for you to choose from?

Danson: Langston Hughes Poems, Stories from Africa, Al Gore's movie, moats and castles, fables, Mother Theresa, Bach, Mozart, Beethoven.

February 6
Topic: Langston Hughes

I read Langston Hughes' "I've Known Rivers" aloud and Danson practices his handwriting by answering questions about the poem.

Michele: Let's talk about some of the rivers in this poem. Where is the Congo?

Danson: Africa. Feel it is West.

Michele: Where is the Nile?

Danson: Egypt.

Michele: Do you know where the Euphrates is? I don't.

Danson: Everywhere I go is only my world Mom.

Michele: What is the poet trying to say?

Danson: *(He stops his handwriting practice and uses his letter board)*

Give me a hint.

(I do)

Mom I am not liking this poem. It is not heavy enough.

I read Hughes' "I, Too, Sing America" aloud.

Danson: My brothers are singing songs of no freedom in the world. I Too Am America means home is not liking my history. Man is so young in the life of my story. Have not yet sold out on the lost honor for making the most of life in America. Right now I miss my grandmother. List me her likes. She likes my movies too. Half notice her here now so I am falling alive. Right now the only voice I hear is you. I hear your voice in my slow motor style. It sounds like a lion roaring to me. You are strong in my hearing.

Michele: Does that mean I am talking loud or that we have a strong connection?

Danson: That means we are one in the same.

(He becomes very agitated)

Hitting a wall is hard for me. Mom I am not giving up. I am climbing higher everyday. Have love for me always and do not stop making me work hard.

February 7
Topic: Castles and Moats

We read excerpts from a book on castles and moats. Danson seems distracted and doesn't want to do a lesson or sit down.

Michele: What is an archer?

Danson: An archer is a man with a bow and arrow.

Michele: Where did people who lived in castles store their food?

Danson: In a basement.

Michele: Yes, it was called a keep and, as we read, the thick stone walls and closeness to the well where they got water kept food cold. It is 2008. If Hedingham Castle was built in 1440 and still stands, how old is it now?

Danson starts fighting and kicking.

Danson: Mom, I am so lost in thought. My mind has left my body like I'm not in control of it. Not sure why. Mom I am staying home. Give me my space to write my story in my head first. Hindsight is twenty twenty. Roaring in your talking is hard to do in forced intervals. Make my skool in my head real, not insomuch as a place but in a life mission….It would work best to make my lessons in a morning like Mom is my teacher now in school. A moat is for protecting a castle from harm.

Michele: So even when you are kicking and screaming you are still listening!?

Danson: Yes, I still hear. Mom I need enough sleep to learn. My God was talking to me last night.

Michele: Will you sleep tonight?

Danson: Only if I can make my God quiet. My God is not real in this world. He loves.

February 8
Topic: Alternative Energy Sources

Danson does not want to do lessons today and runs upstairs. I read a little to him from a book on alternative energy sources, then ask Mike to read, thinking Danson might be more responsive to him.

Mike: What kind of fuel is primarily used today?

Danson: Fossal.

Mike: What are two other energy sources we read about?

Danson: Wind and water.

Mike writes a question on paper: "Does hot air rise or fall?" Danson picks "rise." Mike then writes, "Where is wind harvested? A wind tunnel or wind farm?" Danson picks "wind farm."

At school that morning, we meet Marilyn Chadwick of Facilitated Communication Institute, Syracuse University. Danson goes to the keyboard and types: TEACH ME HOW TO TALK.

February 9
Topic: Writing

Again today, Danson does not want to do his lesson.

Michele: So Danson, what's on your mind today?

Danson: No one taught me how to talk today. Lift my voice to the hills to praise. Foolish games for little outcome are my lot and I am so tired of trying so hard to talk and I am like a hot field for reform in education and I feel my rights are compromised.

Be my mom and not force me to work all the time at my writing. Mike is hard on me and I like it. Mike are you my friend? Mike are you mad at my mom a lot of the time for showing more attention to me than you? My knowledge of marriage makes me ask if love is forever.

Danson is avoiding having to work on his lesson and starts playing around. I ask why he is fighting so much every day, and tell him that if he wants to end his lessons we can. But I explain that we want to teach him so he can express all of his brilliant thoughts and have rich relationships and go to college, if he wants to one day. I talk about the people we've learned about who had autism and were misunderstood because of it – like Larry, a man who was sent to an institution at first.

Now, as an adult, he's learned to type and he lives a full and happy life on his own; he even has his own art studio.

Danson: Life is not good in an institution. Right now I am so mad about my... (He doesn't finish the sentence). Will my mom not stay with me in life and I have to be alone?

Michele: I will always love you and always be with you, as long as I am alive.

While meeting with a new potential caregiver for Danson today, Danson spells, "Friends are my specialty. Are you my friend?" He gives her a kiss when she leaves.

February 11
Topic: Writing

Once again, Danson does not want to do his lesson and fights with me throughout. I read these words from Don Miguel Ruiz' The Four Agreements aloud: "Speak with Integrity. Say only what you mean. Avoid using the word against yourself or to gossip about others. Use the power of your word in the direction of truth and love."

Michele: Danson, what do you think of this quote?

Danson: Integrity means being honest. Mom I need a chance to see my next step to write my story in my head. I am giving my rights away. I bothered Mom in my sarcasm. I don't want to make my master speaking. Have to learn how to type too. I typed in school today.

Michele: That's great Danson! Do you like typing with Lisa at school?

Danson: I am giving it my best. I am a leader in skool.

Michele: Yes you are!

(He is becoming agitated again)

Michele: Do you want to stop your lessons? It seems like every day is a fight.

Danson: I do not want to stop my lessons. I need to learn many more things. I hate feeling so mad.

February 13
Topic: Writing

*Finally, Danson is happy and wants to do his lesson. It's a snow day
– is there a connection?*

*I read a quote from E. M. Forster: "We must be willing to let go of
the life we have planned so as to have the life that is waiting for us."
I give Danson three choices on paper: "Do you want to talk about
this quote? Your upcoming vacation plans? Or something else?" He
chooses "something else."*

Danson: I want to talk about my skool. I go to skool at
Celebrate the Children. It is like jumping my mind.
It is my Lisa place so I love it. She is keeping me on
my toes. Lisa making me type in skool is my riting
style. I like living in New Jersey because I see myself
giving my stories to Mom here. I learned riting on the
computer this week. My mom teaches me in every
element.

Michele: Danson, I really want to talk with you about something important. You know how me and Mike and Daddy and Marysa go to see Dr. McCurtis to learn more about how we can work together and help you? After a lot of talking and research, we have found a medication that might help you feel more calm and less anxious and I want to know how you feel about that. Many people in the world, including your parents, have taken medication before to get through times of great anxiety or depression. Are you interested in trying something like that to see if it helps you feel better?

Danson: Yes I would like to try it.

Michele: The trial would be for 30 days. Will you tell us how you feel every day?

Danson: Yes I will.

Michele: Do you understand what this is all for?

Danson: Anxiety.

We discuss his upcoming vacation with Dad and how much fun they will have swimming and playing together. We talk about how it will be for him being at a hotel for two days with Dad and then at his Brooklyn home for two days with Dad and Marysa. Danson picks up a pencil and writes on a piece of paper: WESTIN PRINCETON. I LIKE THE HEAVENLY BED.

February 21
At Celebrate the Children School

Morning hysterics while Danson kicks, screams and scratches, and I yell too. It is awful for all of us. Danson throws a cup of juice containing his medication and then goes to his letter board and writes: "Mad at Mom for making me take medicine. It makes me feel like I am sick in the head."

At CTC today, Danson throws himself around and continues screaming. Lisa takes Danson to her car where it is quiet and isolated. There, he finds a big Hershey's kiss that fascinates him.

Lisa has a "chocolate drawer" in her desk where she keeps treats. A few days ago Danson sat down at her desk to find the drawer empty. So, yesterday morning when he walked into school, he put his Kit Kat in the drawer, and after finishing his lunch, he went back over to get it. It's a funny little insight into Danson's lovely logic, as well as his ability to retain information – some have questioned whether he can.

Lisa: Do you want to talk about chocolate or medicine?

Danson: Medicine.

Lisa: How does it make you feel?

Danson: Too soon to tell.

Lisa: Right this minute, how do you feel?

Danson: Slow. Scary.

Lisa: Slower is different for you, but not necessarily bad. Dr. McCurtis wants you to try this for 30 days to see if it can make you feel good and less anxious. Does slow have to be scary?

Danson: Yes, you are right.

Lisa: What might help you sleep better?

Danson: Rocking with stones.

Lisa thinks Danson is referring to the rose quartz I give him to hold sometimes as a reminder of unconditional love.

Lisa: Anything else you want to say?

Danson: I would like some water please.

Danson has since settled into a very low dosage of anti-anxiety medication that helps him sleep, but may potentially cause him to lose some focus during his academic work. We are monitoring his focus and anxiety daily. Everything comes down to balance and communication.

March 16
Topic: Family

Danson has been kicking and fighting a lot today. We discuss Daddy and Marysa's soon-to-be baby daughter. Somehow, Danson knew it would be a girl before anyone else. I am often struck by his "knowingness."

Danson: I am mad about my sister because I am an only child and I am not sure how it will be for me now.

Michele: What questions do you have?

Danson: Will my sister have my hair too?

Will she give my mom love too?

Find myself thinking about my future a lot. Give me my music now. Pleasing to my life – my solomn youth.

Mom I am not saying why I scratch anymore. Fights are not bad. I have good intentions for myself. My mind has to make my right fingers listen to it. Hot now so I am not writing.

Michele: Dad and Marysa are always going to love you and you'll always be Daddy's #1 boy!

Danson: Mom are you going to have a baby too?

Michele: I don't think so, why?

Danson: I'm a little glad.

Michele: What else is on your mind today?

Danson: *He says "book!" aloud, and then writes:*
My book is making me lots of love in the world. I dedicate my book to God and all who read it.

Michele: Time for school now.

Danson: Skool is my game to play now.

March 17
On Our Way to Celebrate the Children

When we arrive at school, Danson is upset, as he has been for many days, and doesn't want to get out of the car. I tell him whatever he needs educationally, we will figure it out, and all he has to do is talk to me. I tell him that in the past we did not understand his mind, but now that we are starting to, he will be an equal participant in his own future.

Danson: I have to think about it.

He is quiet for a moment, then:

Mom, you are the right mom for me.

April 1
Topic: Saturn

I read to Danson from the new book, The Universe.

Michele: How many moons does Saturn have?

Danson: 33 moons.

Michele: How wide is Saturn and do you prefer to answer in miles or kilometers?

Danson: A mile is a more masterful measurement.

Michele: OK! So, how many miles wide is Saturn?

Danson: 150,000 miles

Michele: Is Saturn a large or small planet?

Danson: Saturn is the second largest planet in the solar system. My next book is in my head already.

Michele: What is it about?

Danson: History of my salvation.

April 2
Topic: Swahili and Typing

I ask Danson to choose between reading about the cosmos or learning some Kiswahili. *He chooses Swahili.*

We review the following words:

Jambo – *hello*
Habari gani – *how are you?*
Nzuri sana – *very fine*
Tafadali – *please*
Mzee – *a wise elder*
Rafiki yongu – *my friend*

Danson watches my mouth very closely and repeats the sounds aloud. Then he changes the subject.

Danson: I want to talk about Austin. When will we move? I want to move there next August please.

Michele: Why?

Danson: To go to my skool in September. My skool has a lot of computers.

Michele: Do you know how to type on a computer?

Danson: Yes I do, with help.

Just lately I have come downstairs to find Danson quietly sitting at my desk, facing my laptop. I know that he is teaching himself to type – though he is not yet laying his hands on the keys. Like he did with the letterboard, when he is ready, he will probably begin his actual typing with full, complete sentences. Right now, typing letter by letter is hard and requires a lot of guidance, meaning that he has not yet developed the fine motor skill of pushing the letters accurately. Danson is so very independent and does not like learning new things that challenge him, but inevitably, he will master those challenges and only then will he share them with others.

"you are the right mom for me"

Those words marked a subtle yet profound turning point for Danson and me. In that moment on that March day, I truly understood that we had, in effect, come to an agreement – one of total, loving respect for each other's wisdom. I believe that Danson came to this place of understanding as well. Though there are times when we and Danson disagree, he is and will always be an empowered, equal participant in all decisions that affect his life.

June 9
Topic: Standing on the Shoulders of Giants

Michele: Today we discussed one of your family members and also the concept of standing on the shoulders of giants. What does that phrase mean to you?

Danson: It means our ancestors are great men and women. Tell me about my grandfather Bunche.

Michele: I make some comments about Ralph Johnson Bunche's major accomplishments at the United Nations, his educational history, meeting grandmommy, establishing the political science department at Howard University etc. Then I ask, what stands out the most for you from hearing the story of Ralph Bunche?

Danson: He was a man of peace in the world.

Michele: How was he acknowledged worldwide as a peace maker?

Danson: Nobel Peace Prize.

Michele: Yes, and he was the first Black man in history to receive that honor. Who was the second?

Danson: Martin Luther King.

Michele: Yes! And where did Dr. Bunche study?

Danson: UCLA and Harvard.

Michele: Where do you want to study, do you know yet?

Danson: (no answer) Want to study math. Mom is really mean to me. I'm in elementary school and you treat me like I'm in college. I want you to tell me a story about my mailman. Write me a story so I can read.

Michele: Danson, you know I challenge you because you are brilliant and I want to engage your mind – I do it because I believe in you, not to be mean. Anyway, can you tell me anything special about your mailman, like what is his name?

Danson: Mr. or Mrs. X.

Michele: So our story begins, "No one knew where Mr. X went each morning at 5:37 am, since his mail route began at noon…"

June 25

It's Danson's last day of school before summer break and his teacher Lisa just called saying he was having a fit. He'd just written: "I'm so sad" and then said aloud "so sad" as the tears streamed down his little face. When she asked why he was sad, he wrote: "I will miss you. I love you." She said she loved him too, and will see him at camp this summer. They hugged and cried together, and then he wrote: "it takes a special person to love me." Then Lisa responded "Danson, you are very easy to love."

*S*o, *how is Danson doing, as we go to press? Since Danson finished his book, he continues being both brilliant and a child, and we're learning together. As always, he's the one who puts things into perspective and brings me back. At the end of the day he's just like the millions of children (and adults!) around the world: he longs for fun stories, connection—and love.*

Peaceful Sleep Meditation

I speak these words to Danson as he goes to bed each night, but they are for all children, too.

I love everything about you!
Thank you for your smile.
Thank you for your love.
May the angels surround you tonight, my child.
May you sleep in perfect peace
Knowing that you are safe, and loved, and honored.

Dream big tonight, my child
The world is yours!
Never forget that you are blessed
And divinely led,
Meaning within you, you have the ability
To achieve all of your dreams
And you make this world a better place.
You make everyone you meet more loving
And accepting of others and of themselves.
You make me the happiest person in the world.
You are a blessing and I thank God every single day
For placing you in my life.

(A CD of this meditation and the "peaceful sleep" music that accompanies it can be found on our website, www.dansonsbook.com)

About Michele

୬ঌৄ৶

Michele Pierce Burns is a consultant, writer and public speaker, focusing on autism aware-ness and acceptance. She is Director of Development for Celebrate the Children (Wharton, NJ), a state-approved private school for children on the autism spectrum. Previously, she was an elementary and high school teacher and has co-founded two charter schools and a summer academy. She holds a BA from Wesleyan University (English/Afro-American Studies), an MA from Stanford University (Education), and a Master of Education degree from Harvard University (Administration, Planning, and Social Policy). She has been featured on Oprah, The Today Show, and Larry King Live, discussing autism. In print, she can be seen in Essence, Black Enterprise, and big apple parent.

Michele is the proud mother of Danson Mandela Wambua. Besides being co-author of this book, she is currently completing a book dedicated to Danson, called I Love Everything About You, which affirms the idea that a child with autism is a perfect blessing just as he or she is. She and Danson are featured in the documentary film Autism Every Day, which premiered at the 2007 Sundance Film Festival.

Michele volunteers as a member of the Family Services committee at Autism Speaks. She is a certified instructor in yoga and yoga for the special child, and is also a Reiki Master. She is grateful to share her life with Danson and her beautiful husband, Michael.

Michele and Danson can be reached on the web at: www.dansonsbook.com

About Danson

Danson Mandela Wambua is a 9-year-old boy with the heart and mind of a poet. Until Danson was eighteen months old, he appeared to be a healthy, attentive, affectionate and highly-focused baby. But after struggling with a severe respiratory condition that placed him in ICU for several days, his demeanor changed dramatically and he became listless and withdrawn. He no longer responded to his name or made any attempt to speak. We don't know if the illness was related to his autism, but Danson was eventually diagnosed as "non-verbal autistic."

At 7, Danson began therapy at the HALO Clinic in Austin, Texas, where at last he discovered a way to communicate, by pointing to letters on an alphabet board. Almost immediately, he began sharing not only his feelings (love for his family) and desires (an iPod and jeans), but also his spiritual and intellectual yearnings (to understand faith, and to be challenged by complex ideas and concepts). One day in August, after a brief lesson about poetry, Danson wrote his own first poem, and he has not stopped since.

Along with poetry, he is highly skilled at mathematics, swimming and nearly any activity that captures his imagination. His other interests include horseback riding, music (especially Mozart) and hiking. He lives in New Jersey with his mother and stepfather, Michele Pierce Burns and Michael Burns, and in Brooklyn with his father and stepmother, Mathew and Marysa Wambua. He currently attends Celebrate the Children in New Jersey, after having been home schooled for 2 years.

Danson has appeared (in video) on Oprah and Larry King Live, and was featured with his mother in the documentary film Autism Every Day, in 2006. His words give voice to an amazing spirit, one made of limitless love, deep wisdom and beauty, and – sometimes – sadness.

ACKNOWLEDGMENTS

From Michele: Danson, every single moment with you is a blessing, every smile you share a gift. Thank you for taking my breath away on a daily basis. To Mathew, for having such a pure and infinite love for your son, for smiling so broadly every single time you have ever walked in—in each of those instances looking at him like the miraculous moment he was born, and for the love that we will always share as a family. To Marysa, thank you for loving Danson so deeply – for thinking about him every day, for emailing your beautiful letters to him expressing your innermost thoughts, for always being the first to reply so thoughtfully to my messages and sometimes cries for help. To Danson's new baby sister Zaharek Mahalia Wambua, we love you and welcome you with open hearts and arms! And to Michael, you have chosen a daily life that is far from easy. You put me and Danson first in your life every single day and you have helped create the loving home in which so many of these incredible words were born. Your love calms storms and makes everything right. Thank you for dancing around the living room with us as we laugh until we cry.

To Paul, Catherine, Abby, and St. Lynn's Press, I cry when I type your names because you are the angels who believed in us from moment one and honored Danson every step of the way!

Infinite love and gratitude to all our families: Pierce, Wambua, Burns, Kjellson, Sutton and Taylor. And especially mommy and daddy: you have given me everything and if I am 1/10th the parent to Danson that you are/were to me, he will be the luckiest boy in the world. To Soma, thank you for the greatest gift we ever received: the ability to talk with Danson and hear his voice. To Monica and our CTC family, we thank you and love you so.

Suzanne and Bob, thank you for roaring so loudly for all our children! For everyone in Danson's life who has so consistently and powerfully loved him, seen beauty and possibility in him, dreamed about him and prayed for him, and most of all always believed in him... You know who you are and Danson does too. Bless You. He heard you all along.

POSTSCRIPT: September. *Danson's new baby sister Zaharek was born in August. Like most children, Danson had some apprehensions about becoming a big brother after eight years of undivided attention! Soon after, Mathew and Marysa asked Danson to write about his feelings, as he so often feels better once he gets things off his chest.*

Zaharek you worry me.
You are beautiful.
You worry me.
You are unbelievable
You worry me
You are powerful
You worry me
You are wonderful
You worry me
You are Zaharek
You worry me
You are pure
You worry me
You are Zaharek
You worry me.

Love Danson, Your Brother.

Danson's daddy told him that this was a beautiful poem that touched them both, and said that great art has the capacity to elicit different meanings and emotions in its readers. Marysa added that the poem almost perfectly articulated her current emotions towards Zaharek. To which Danson replied, "Yes, great art is transcendent."

RESOURCES

∽☙∾

Below is a list of the programs/therapies/experiences we recommend, most of which we have done with Danson. This is by no means an exhaustive list, just a beginning, for further exploration. Of course, every child and every child with autism is different, so we are not saying these are the best or only ways to go – simply sharing what is working for our family. Many of these programs and individuals below have been VERY generous to our family, offering pro-bono services or discounted rates when needed. We are so grateful! (Additional resources can be found on our website: www.dansonsbook.com)

Helping Autism through Learning and Outreach (HALO)

www.HALO-Soma.org

HALO is a non-profit organization in Austin, Texas, dedicated to the use of Soma Mukhopadhyay's Rapid Prompting™ Method (Soma® RPM), for persons with autism and similar communication challenges to improve academic success and communication. Soma engages Danson intellectually like no one ever has, and challenges him each time he is with her to do breakthrough communication. Soma originally created RPM for her son Tito, now 19, who has just published his 3rd enlightening book *How Can I Talk If My Lips Don't Move?* After reading Tito's first book, *The Mind Tree*, which he wrote between the ages of 8-11, I first realized that a "non-verbal" autistic person could be an absolute genius, with savant qualities. It is then that I changed my language from "low-functioning" or "severely autistic" to "gifted" or "genius" when referring to my son or those like him.

RPM uses quick-paced question prompting to academic material to initiate a student's independent response. There is a fierce commitment to presuming intelligence, and in every case I have seen, the student rises to the occasion. Year-round "camps" are offered in Austin during which a child works one-on-one with Soma and her apprentice in two 40-minute sessions per day. Additionally, HALO offers week-long RPM training to parents and educators to learn the method. Caution: people from ages 5-60 come from all over the world to see Soma, so the wait list can be quite long (up to a year). I volunteer to support the organization by writing grants so that the apprentice program can grow in expertise and there will be others qualified to do RPM with our children.

In addition to teaching letter-chart pointing, RPM also utilizes stencils and other drawing exercises to lead to independent handwriting.

Celebrate the Children (CTC), Wharton, NJ

www.celebratethechildren.org

I first read about Celebrate the Children (CTC) in TIME Magazine when there was an autism cover story (May, 2006). The images of children laughing and connecting with staff members in such a strong, obvious, and loving way stayed in my mind for weeks, so much so that I began having dreams of Danson there. CTC is a state-approved private school for children ages 4-17 with alternative learning styles. It is based upon the relationship-based Floortime model created by Dr. Stanley Greenspan. Founder Monica Osgood writes: "People who have difficulty processing sensory information see, hear, feel, smell, and taste information at both higher and lower intensities than people without these processing problems. Because we receive all information though our senses, these processing difficulties often lead to misperceptions of information, under- or over-stimulation, disregulation and sometimes, anxiety." The number one priority at CTC is to help students learn how to self-regulate so they can get out of a constant "fight or flight" mode and open up to learning.

Autism Speaks

www.autismspeaks.org

Autism Speaks is dedicated to funding global biomedical research into the causes, prevention, treatments, and cure for autism; to raising public awareness about autism and its effects on individuals, families, and society; and to bringing hope to all who deal with the hardships of this disorder. They are committed to raising the funds necessary to support these goals. Autism Speaks aims to bring the autism community together as one strong voice to urge the government and private sector to listen to our concerns and take action to address this urgent global health crisis. Co-Founders Bob and Suzanne Wright, named one of the TIME 100 Heroes and Pioneers for 2007, are exactly that. I am inspired by them on a daily basis and grateful to Suzanne beyond words for her love and mentorship. Autism Speaks offers many, many resources and programs to families free of charge.

Starlight Farms

www.starlightfarms.org

Starlight Farms (Ringwood, NJ) provides equine-assisted activities and therapies to individuals with disabilities – promoting the healing power of the horse-human connection. The goals are to encourage positive self-esteem, confidence and independence in the relaxing, enjoyable setting of the farm. This has been an extremely calming and positive experience for Danson.

Prompt Speech Therapy

www.promptinstitute.com

The PROMPT Institute is a non-profit organization dedicated to investigating and promoting holistic, dynamic, multi-sensory assessment and interventions for individuals with speech production disorders. The organization's mission is to provide workshops and education for speech-language pathologists, caregivers and the general public on PROMPT and speech production disorders. PROMPT has been the best form of speech therapy for Danson.

The Autism Treatment Center of America/Son Rise Program

www.autismtreatmentcenter.org

Central to any of Danson's growth has been our total acceptance of him. We did three week-long parent trainings and a week-long intensive with Danson at the beautiful campus in Sheffield, MA. This was the basis of our home-school program and I recommend it to every parent everywhere.

Syracuse University Facilitated Communication Institute

http://thefci.syr.edu/index.html

I am very impressed by what I've seen of Facilitated Communication, and Institute Director Marilyn Chadwick has recently begun consulting at Danson's school. The teachers and speech therapists are excited about beginning this new methodology which is similar in many ways to RPM – the difference being that a physical prompt is used in addition to a verbal prompt (such as a hand on the shoulder or elbow of writer to help them locate their bodies in space etc.) This website offers many wonderful training opportunities for parents and educators.

Water Planet Dolphin Camp

www.waterplanetusa.com

We have always wanted to take Danson to swim with the dolphins at Panama City Beach, FL. The Directors have been VERY warm and generous to us in the many phone calls we have had working to set this up for Danson. One day we'll get there!

FlagHouse Inc./Snoozelen

www.flaghouse.com

This is a phenomenal company for therapeutic products and design of the most incredible sensory experiences I have ever seen. Danson wrote that one of their weighted vests was "a little piece of heaven" and that it made him feel "safe." At my request, FlagHouse has recently partnered with Celebrate the Children to design state-of-the-art sensory rooms.

Yoga, Meditation, Wellness

Henry L. McCurtis, MD

A New York City-based psychiatrist, Dr. McCurtis is like a member of our family and our chief advisor. All four of Danson's parents sit with him once a month for hours at a time and we have the most productive conversations about Danson imaginable. Dr. McCurtis has a private practice and for many years was Director, department of psychiatry, Harlem Hospital and Assistant Professor of Clinical Psychiatry at Columbia College of Physicians and Surgeons.

Yoga for the Special Child

www.yogaforthespecialchild.com

Yoga for the Special Child®, LLC is a comprehensive program of yoga techniques designed to enhance the natural development of children with special needs. This style of yoga is gentle and therapeutic – safe for babies and children with Down Syndrome, Cerebral Palsy, Microcephaly, Autism and other developmental disabilities. These methods also provide an effective treatment for children diagnosed with Attention Deficit Disorder, ADHD and Learning Disabilities. Founder Sonia Sumar is one of the finest teachers I have ever had. Just being around her makes you feel good! She has taught me much about yoga and much about life.

Aleta St. James

www.aletastjames.com

Aleta is a world-renowned healer and success coach, who uses her Energy Transformation System™ to help you to rapidly release and awaken your higher self at a cellular level. Aleta has three meditation CD's that we listen to often; her voice is like an angel's. Danson connects with Aleta in an extraordinary way that is difficult to describe in words. She is a generous and gentle spirit, a healing presence in our lives.

American Yoga Academy/Claire Diab

www.americanyogaacademy.com

The American Yoga Academy teaches people a gentle safe and effective way to create balance and harmony within themselves, which simultaneously fosters harmony in their outer world as well. I love Claire Diab and have completed yoga teacher training with her and assisted her in this class. Michael and I practiced with her together in private sessions, and she is a master – her eyes sparkle!

The Chopra Center

www.chopra.com

What can be said about Dr. Deepak Chopra? Many of the beliefs and attitudes I mention in this book are informed by my studies at the Chopra Center. Michael and I read Deepak's books aloud to one another and to Danson, and his chakra balancing CD is my all-time favorite. Deepak taught me that it is as if Danson is listening to another frequency on the radio and most of us can't hear it. It's that simple.

∽❂〜

A PPS. FROM MICHELE: *Here's what Danson wrote on July 18, as I showed him a photo of the 25 acres we are looking to purchase for his home school program. He laughed, squealed, and wrote:*

> I am excited about my almost school.
> I am deleriously alive!